Level
2

THE NATURE KIDS GUIDE TO

SHARKS

DAVID ANDERSON

For information address LP Media Inc. Publishing,
30012 Variolite St NW, Princeton MN 55371
www.lpmedia.org

Publication Data

Sharks
The Nature Kid's Guide to Sharks — First edition.

Summary: "Learn all about Sharks, the Nature Kid Way"
— Provided by publisher.

ISBN: 979-8-89818-102-4

[1. Sharks – Non-Fiction] I. Title.

Title: The Nature Kid's Guide to Sharks

CONTENTS

SALTY SEAS

Sharks have lived in Earth's oceans for over 400 million years. That means sharks existed before dinosaurs walked on land!

Whoosh! A shark glides through the ocean. Its strong tail pushes it forward.

Sharks live in salty ocean water. They need salt water to survive. The ocean covers most of Earth and is home to many shark species.

Sharks live in different parts of the ocean. Some swim near the surface, while others stay deep below. The water can be warm or cold.

Many sharks stay near coasts. Coral reefs and rocky shores both have lots of sharks. Other sharks swim in the open sea far from land or **migrate** across the oceans.

Sharks breathe through gills. Water flows over the gills, which take oxygen from the water.

SHARKS EVERYWHERE

Great white sharks can travel across entire oceans. Some swim 12,000 miles yearly.

Splash! A Reef shark swims in warm tropical water.

Sharks live in oceans all around the world. Great white sharks cruise the cool waters off California and South Africa. Whale sharks glide through warm tropical seas near Mexico.

Some sharks live in surprising places. Greenland sharks swim in freezing Arctic waters under the ice. Bull sharks can even swim up freshwater rivers far from the ocean!

Different sharks have found homes in almost every kind of water on Earth. From shallow coral reefs to the deepest, darkest parts of the ocean, sharks are everywhere.

SUPER
SIZED

Snap! A whale shark opens its huge mouth wide. It could swallow a car!

Sharks come in many sizes. Whale sharks are the largest fish species. They can grow longer than a school bus.

But some sharks are very small. Dwarf lantern sharks fit in a human hand. They are only about six inches long.

Most sharks are medium-sized, though. Ranging from 6 to 12 feet long. Great white sharks can reach 20 feet long.

Dwarf lantern sharks live deep in the ocean where it's pitch black. Their bellies glow in the dark to help them hide from predators swimming below!

SHARP SMILES

Chomp! A shark bites down hard. Its teeth are razor sharp.

Sharks have rows of sharp teeth. When one tooth falls out, another moves forward to replace it. Some sharks grow thousands of teeth in their lifetime.

Different sharks have different teeth shapes. Great white sharks have triangle teeth with jagged edges. This helps them cut through food.

Other sharks have flat teeth instead. These crush the hard shells of crabs and clams. The shape matches what each shark eats.

Shark teeth contain fluoride, like toothpaste. This makes them extra strong!

SUPER
SENSORS

A shark senses something nearby. It turns to investigate.

Sharks have amazing senses. They can detect things that other animals cannot.

Sharks smell very well. They can detect one drop of blood from far away. Their nostrils work only for smelling.

Sharks also sense electricity. Special pores on their snouts feel tiny electric signals. Fish give off these electric signals. This helps the sharks hunt them.

Sharks can hear low sounds from far away that humans cannot hear!

TOUGH SKIN

Dermal denticles means "skin teeth" in Latin. They're made like shark teeth!

DID YOU KNOW?

Swoosh! A shark brushes past a rock. Its skin feels like sandpaper.

Shark skin is very tough. It protects sharks from scratches and bites, helping keep them safe. Unlike bony fish, sharks have skeletons made of **cartilage** — the same bendy material in your nose and ears!

Shark skin is covered with tiny scales. These scales are called **dermal denticles**. They feel rough like sandpaper.

The scales all point toward the tail. This shape helps water flow smoothly over the body. Smoother water flow can help sharks swim more efficiently.

FEEDING FRENZY

Crunch! A shark bites into a Lionfish. Dinner is served.

Sharks eat many different foods. Most sharks eat fish and squid. Some eat seals or sea turtles too.

Whale sharks are the biggest fish in the ocean. But they only eat tiny **plankton**!

Tiger sharks eat almost anything they find.

Sharks do not chew their food. Instead, they bite off chunks and swallow them whole. Their sharp teeth help them grab prey. Some sharks can go weeks between meals.

Tiger sharks eat almost anything. They have been caught with tires and license plates in the stomaches!

SNEAK ATTACK

Snarl! A Great White shark lurks in murky water, waiting for its prey.

Many sharks are sneaky hunters. They use surprise to catch their food, and different sharks have different tricks.

Great white sharks attack from below. They swim up fast and hit their prey hard. This knocks the animal into the air.

Thresher sharks use their long tails. They whip their tails to stun fish. Then they eat the dizzy fish.

Some sharks hide on the ocean floor. Wobbegongs look like rocks and seaweed, so fish swim close without knowing. Then the shark strikes fast.

BIG BULLIES

Thump! A big shark bumps a smaller one. The smaller shark swims away.

Some sharks push other sharks around. Bigger sharks often bully smaller ones. They bump them to show who is boss.

Sharks also use body language to communicate. A shark might arch its back. It might lower its fins. These moves warn other sharks to stay away.

Bigger sharks sometimes steal food from smaller sharks. The small shark usually swims off. It knows better than to fight a bigger shark.

Bull sharks are very aggressive. They headbutt prey before biting!

21

SWIM AWAY

A Mako shark spots danger. It darts away fast.

Sharks have ways to escape danger. Larger sharks, orcas, and even people can scare them away. Their powerful tails help them flee quickly.

Sharks sense trouble before it arrives. They feel vibrations in the water. This helps them know when to leave.

Some sharks swim to deeper water to hide. Others head to kelp forests or reefs. These places offer safety.

Mako sharks can leap 20 feet out of the water when escaping danger or chasing prey.

24

Flash! A mako shark races through the sea. It zooms past fish.

Some sharks are built for speed. Their bodies are shaped like torpedoes. This helps them cut through water easily.

Mako sharks are the fastest sharks. They zoom ahead in short, quick bursts. Their pointed snouts help them slice through the water.

Some sharks swim slowly to save energy. Then they burst forward to catch food.

Mako sharks can swim up to 45 miles per hour. That's faster than most boats can go!

25

LAZY DAYS

Zzzzzz... A nurse shark rests on the sandy ocean floor.

Some sharks rest during the day. This helps them save energy for nighttime hunting. Nurse sharks often lie still on the sandy bottom.

Many sharks must keep swimming to breathe. Water flows over their **gills** as they move. These sharks may slow down while resting, but they never fully stop.

Some sharks rest in caves or under ledges. These spots offer shade and protection.

Nurse sharks can pump water over their gills. This lets them breathe without swimming, unlike most other sharks.

SOLO SWIMMERS

A Bull shark swims alone in the deep blue sea. It hunts by itself.

Many sharks swim and hunt alone. Others like to be together.

Some sharks gather together near food sources. These groups may last a short time. But some stay together longer.

Hammerhead sharks sometimes swim in large groups called schools. Scientists are still learning why they form these big groups.

Hammerhead sharks can gather in groups of over 500 during the day but hunt alone at night.

FINDING FRIENDS

A male shark spots a female and follows close behind.

Special signals help males find females. Female sharks release chemicals into the water. Males can smell these signals from far away.

When a male finds a female, he follows her closely. They swim together before mating. The male sometimes bites the female's fins to hold on.

Sharks gather in certain areas to mate. These spots have warm water and plenty of food.

After mating, female sharks can wait many months before having babies. Their bodies wait until the time is right to become pregnant.

PUNY
PUPS

Squeak! A tiny shark pup swims for the first time.

Baby sharks swim right after birth. They are born small but ready to swim. Most pups take care of themselves right away.

Some sharks lay eggs in cases. These cases are called mermaid's purses. The eggs stay safe on the ocean floor until they hatch.

Other sharks give birth to live pups. Some pups grow inside their mother for up to two years. Lemon shark pups, for example, are about two feet long when born.

Shark pups are born with a full set of teeth. They're ready to hunt small fish and crabs from day one!

GO SOLO

DID YOU KNOW?
Shark nursery areas can be near mangroves or coral reefs.

Snort! A mother shark swims off. Her pups are on their own.

Shark parents do not care for their young. Pups must survive alone from the start. They are born knowing how to swim and hunt.

Mother sharks leave after giving birth. They do not feed or protect their babies. So pups hide in shallow waters called nurseries.

These nursery areas have fewer big sharks. Young sharks can find small fish to eat. They stay until they grow larger.

Some pups travel far from where they were born.

SCARY SEAS

Oh no! A whale shark swallows a piece of floating trash!

Pollution is a big danger to sharks. Plastic fills the oceans and sharks sometimes eat this garbage by mistake.

Chemicals from farms and factories also wash into the water, poisoning the places where sharks live and hunt.

People are a threat to sharks too. Every year, poachers illegally kill millions of sharks just for their fins. The fins are sold for lots of money, even though this cruel practice is against the law in many countries.

SAVING SHARKS

Buzz! Scientists attach a tracker to a shark's fin.

Many people work to save sharks. Scientists study where sharks swim. This helps protect important ocean areas.

Some countries make laws to stop people from catching too many sharks. Marine parks give sharks safe places to live.

You can help too. Never buy shark fin products. Pick up beach trash. Tell friends why sharks matter.

Shark fin soup was once so popular in Asia that 100 million sharks were killed each year just for their fins

GLOSSARY

gills
Body parts that help sharks breathe by taking oxygen from water.

dermal denticles
Tiny rough scales that cover a shark's skin like sandpaper.

plankton
Very tiny living things that float in the ocean.

migrate
To travel a long way to find food or better weather.

cartilage
Bendy material that makes up a shark's skeleton, like the stuff in your nose.